STORIES
of the
Aurora

DOT TO DOT IN THE SKY

STORIES of the Aurora

JOAN MARIE GALAT

ILLUSTRATED BY
LORNA BENNETT

whitecap

EDITOR: Patrick Geraghty
DESIGN: Diane Robertson
PROOFREADER: Abby Wiseman

PRINTED IN CANADA.

Library and Archives Canada Cataloguing in Publication
Galat, Joan Marie, 1963-, author

Dot to dot in the sky : stories of the aurora / Joan Marie Galat ; Lorna Bennett, illustrator.
Includes index.

ISBN 978-1-77050-210-9 (paperback)
1. Auroras--Folklore--Juvenile literature. 2. Auroras--Juvenile literature. I. Bennett, Lorna, 1960-, illustrator II. Title.
QC971.4.G35 2015j538'.768C2015-905209-2

Alberta Foundation for the Arts

Canada Council for the Arts   Conseil des arts du Canada

For Gina, who touches my heart,
just like the aurora.
—JOAN

For Emily
and Eliana.
—LORNA

Contents

Acknowledgements

I am very pleased to recognize the frequent and generous assistance given by Douglas Hube, professor emeritus at the University of Alberta and former national president (1994–96) of the Royal Astronomical Society of Canada.

My gratitude extends to Patrick Geraghty, Whitecap Books editor, whose invaluable attention to detail enhanced every aspect of this title. Thank you also to the Alberta Foundation for the Arts for its much appreciated financial support during the research and writing of *Stories of the Aurora*.

J.M.G.

Credit: Sebastian Saarloos

The Mysterious Lights

High in the sky, green, white, red, and purple ribbons of light flicker and wave, as if dancing to the sounds of a celestial choir. It's impossible to predict which way the shimmering, dipping, soaring curtains of light will move next, and this magnificent glow in the sky has inspired many ancient stories as it changes color, shape, and size.

Auroras are created when particles from the Sun enter the Earth's magnetic field and collide with gas in the Earth's atmosphere. In the Northern Hemisphere this amazing show is known as the aurora borealis, or northern lights. In the Southern Hemisphere it is called the aurora australis—southern lights. Most often greenish-white, the lights brighten, fade, and flicker, forming pillars, arches, ribbons, curtains, and haloes of shimmering color in the night sky. The bright bands of light stretch across the heavens from east to west.

The lights were first called "aurora" in the early 1600s, after the Roman goddess Aurora, bringer of the dawn. Some say the Italian scientist Galileo Galilei named them in 1619. Others claim French scientist Pierre Gassendi was the first to use the name "aurora borealis" in 1621. No matter who was first, "aurora" became the scientific term used to describe the mysterious streaks and streamers of light seen in the upper atmosphere, of the magnetic polar regions, of Earth and other planets.

Auroras are only visible from the Earth's northernmost and southernmost regions, and no two are ever alike. People from around the world travel great distances to see the brilliant light displays, which appear without warning high in the Earth's atmosphere. They watch in awe as the lights change colors, ripple, and twirl—a heavenly gift to those who are able to witness them.

Auroras are the closest and most dramatic space phenomena we can see. Since ancient times, their light has amazed and puzzled people. Pictures of auroras have been found in cave drawings, and many cultures believed the lights were connected to the spirit world.

Early peoples both admired and feared the aurora. The scientific explanations we know today had not been developed yet, so ancient cultures told stories to explain why the

Credit: Sebastian Saarloos

mystifying lights appeared in the sky. In areas where auroras were rare, people tended to link them with important events, or perceive them as a warning of something bad that was going to happen. Over time, legends grew—some with happy endings, others ending in disaster. Many stories suggested a connection between people on Earth and powerful gods that lived in a heavenly spirit world.

Science of the Aurora

Understanding auroras begins with understanding some important facts about our Earth and Sun. While you may already know matter can be a solid, liquid, or gas, you may not know it also exists as plasma—matter that is similar to a gas except that the particles are electrically charged. All stars, including our Sun, are made up of plasma, which forms when a gas becomes super heated. Unlike gas, plasma carries electrical currents and generates magnetic fields. Knowing how positively charged particles from the Sun react to the Sun and Earth's magnetic fields makes it easier to understand aurora.

The Earth

The thin outer layer of the Earth is called the crust. The region below the crust is called the mantle and below the mantle is the core. The Earth's core is made up of nickel and iron—metals that can conduct electricity. The inner core is solid, as hot as the Sun's surface, and seventy percent as wide as the Moon. It lies 2,000 miles (3,218 kilometers) below your feet. The outer core is also very hot, but it is liquid. Hot, liquefied metal rises from the bottom of the outer core toward the core's surface. This process is called convection. The combined effect of convection and the Earth's rotation creates electric currents that swirl very slowly within the outer core.

All electric currents generate magnetic fields, and these currents in the Earth create

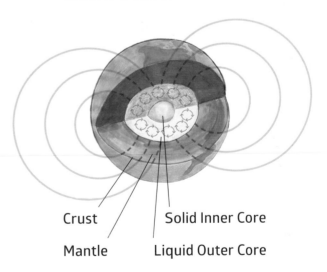

EARTH'S MAGNETIC FIELD

Crust

Mantle

Solid Inner Core

Liquid Outer Core

our planet's magnetic field. The Earth's magnetic field extends through the crust, through the atmosphere (which is made up of

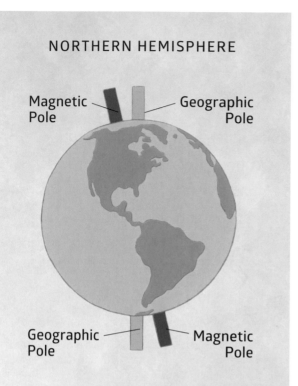

NORTHERN HEMISPHERE

Magnetic Pole

Geographic Pole

Geographic Pole

Magnetic Pole

SOUTHERN HEMISPHERE

Think of the Earth's iron-nickel core as a magnet with one pole pointing north and the other pointing south. The magnetic field is strongest at the Earth's magnetic poles, but it also exists between them. The Earth's magnetic poles are not in the same places as its geographic poles—the imaginary line used to show the axis of the Earth's rotation.

gas molecules—mostly nitrogen and oxygen), and tens of thousands of kilometers out into space. The magnetic field surrounding Earth is known as the magnetosphere.

The upper part of the atmosphere, called the ionosphere, stretches upward from about 37 to 620 miles (60 to 1,000 kilometers). Shaped like a long teardrop, the magnetosphere is the magnetic region that lies within the ionosphere's uppermost region. It reaches about 40,000 miles (64,000 kilometers) into outer space and protects our planet from energetic, electrically charged, subatomic particles.

Auroras occur in the part of the ionosphere that stretches from approximately 45 to 185 miles (70 to 300 kilometers) above Earth. The magnetic field reacts with plasma ejected from the Sun's surface, called the solar wind, and its electrons collide with atoms and ions in the upper atmosphere to create auroras.

The Sun

A luminous ball of gas, 93 million miles (150 million kilometers) away, our Sun contains mostly hydrogen and helium. Its outer atmosphere, called the corona, is made of plasma and stretches more than 620,000 miles (1 million kilometers) from its surface. The Sun's surface temperature is almost 11,000 degrees Fahrenheit (about 6,000 degrees Celsius). It is even hotter on the inside, reaching about 25 million degrees Fahrenheit (14 million degrees Celsius) at its center. This incredible heat forms plasma made up of extremely hot hydrogen and helium.

Near the Sun's center, the extremely high temperature and pressure cause hydrogen nuclei to fuse together in a nuclear reaction that forms helium and releases energy. The motion of the hydrogen and helium atoms in the outer layers of the Sun creates electric currents that generate its magnetic fields.

The magnetic fields on the Sun's surface cause sunspots—strong magnetic regions in the Sun's photosphere (the bright surface layer of the Sun). Most often occurring in groups, sunspots can grow many times larger than the size of Earth. They usually have diameters from about 600 to 30,000 miles (100 to 50,000 kilometers). Sunspots typically last several days but very large ones can last months.

The Sun's magnetic field also causes prominences and flares. Prominences are flame-like eruptions of gas on the Sun's surface, while flares are sudden increases in brightness. Flares release huge amounts of energy and eject plasma at speeds up to a few thousand miles per second.

Sometimes the Sun releases a great explosion of hot plasma called a coronal mass ejection (CME). This happens when bubble-shaped bursts of solar wind form and expand. CMEs can be tens of thousands of miles across and up to tens of millions

Every second, the Sun forms an amount of helium equaling four million tons less than the original amount of hydrogen used to produce it. The hydrogen that disappears is converted into energy, some of which you receive as the light and warmth of sunshine.

of degrees. A single CME might contain a billion tons of matter! Imagine the same mass as Mount Everest being flung toward Earth.

The Sun's outpouring of energy and hot gas, along with the Sun's magnetic fields, creates the solar wind—a flow of charged particles that begins in the corona. Solar wind flows out from the Sun at all times and travels at high speeds—from about 185 miles (300 kilometers) per second to more than 500 miles (800 kilometers) per second. About two to five days after a CME, a small fraction of the plasma flung from the Sun strikes the Earth's magnetic field, causing a magnetic storm as the energetic particles from the Sun are directed by Earth's magnetic field down into the atmosphere. The storm, which can last up to a few days, causes the Earth's magnetic field to vibrate.

The Earth-Sun Connection

Auroras form as charged particles from the Sun react to the Earth's magnetic field. Some of the solar particles follow the magnetic field toward Earth's north and south polar regions. They collide with atoms and molecules in Earth's upper atmosphere and transfer a part of their energy to the atoms and molecules. Beautiful, glowing auroras occur as the gas particles release energy in the form of light.

Each atom or molecule emits a particular color of light. Most auroras display a pale green color from light emitted by oxygen atoms. Oxygen can also create a red edge at the top of an aurora, while nitrogen can create red light along the bottom. The lights may appear white or pale green when faint, and on rare occasions look blue, purple, or a blend of different colors.

Earth's Magnetic Field

- A bubble of magnetism surrounds the Earth. As solar wind flows around the planet, the magnetic field elongates on the night side of Earth to form the 800,000–mile (1.3 million kilometer) long magnetotail. The tail points away from the Sun and stretches beyond the Moon's orbit.

- The Earth's magnetic field stops the Sun's charged particles from directly entering the atmosphere and striking our planet. Some scientists believe Earth would have no water or atmosphere without the magnetosphere.

- The Earth and Sun's magnetic fields meet in an area called the magnetopause.

- Auroras can likely be found on any planet with a magnetic field and atmosphere, if the planet is within range of solar wind. Jupiter, Saturn, Uranus, and Neptune all have auroras because they have magnetic fields and are impacted by the solar wind.

Folklore Around the World

Legends associated with auroras often describe majestic creatures existing both on Earth and above. Finnish and Estonian myths told of a sea monster, possibly a whale, who hit the water with its tail to make beautiful waves of light that rose upward. People who lived in ancient Greenland described the northern lights as a glacier god whose powers could only be seen at night.

Many stories connected auroras to a spirit world. People in northern parts of Canada, Alaska, and Greenland saw the lights as either being alive, or as their ancestor's spirits coming out to show hunters where to find game. In Greenland, auroras were also considered signs from dead relatives and friends who wanted to communicate with those still on Earth. Alaskan Inuit saw the lights as spirits of animals they hunted—seals, salmon, deer, and beluga whales. Northern Aboriginal peoples looked upon auroras as spirit messengers. They believed some men and women could even bring the northern lights lower and make them do their bidding.

Inuit at Alaska's northernmost tip—Point Barrow on the Arctic Ocean—tried to avoid being out at night when the northern lights danced in the sky because they feared auroras could hurt them. If they had to go out, they carried weapons to protect themselves. In Canada's northernmost regions, Inuit thought the northern lights were spirits clothed in mystical lights. They called the fastest moving auroras "the dance of death."

According to folklore in Norway, you could make the lights dance faster by waving a white cloth. In Denmark, the lights were thought to be caused by flapping flocks of geese stuck in ice in the Far North. Their fluttering wings were said to create reflections seen as the northern lights.

Meanwhile, ancient Chinese linked the lights with childbirth, as did many tundra peoples who believed that if the lights appeared as a baby was being born, the mother's pain would be lessened and the child would have a cheerful nature.

In Latvia, close to Russia, a red aurora in the winter meant the souls of dead warriors were fighting. The red curtains of light were believed to warn of war, famine, or other disasters. A more cheerful legend, from nearby Estonia, describes the lights as part of a wedding celebration held in the heavens.

Klondike gold prospectors in North America also took a happier view—they said the northern lights were the reflection of a giant gold deposit.

Other Names for the Aurora

You can often tell what different cultures thought caused the aurora by the names they gave it. People from Finland called auroras revontulet—a Finnish word meaning "fox fire." A Sami legend tells of an arctic fox running across the snow-covered land. If the fox's tail struck the snow, a stream of sparks flew skyward to create an aurora.

In North America's subarctic region, the Chipewyan people knew that rubbing a caribou skin very quickly created sparks, so when they saw auroras, they thought a large herd of caribou must be passing across the sky. They called the northern lights ed-thin, which means "caribou" or "deer."

Some other names used for the aurora translate to:

- Blood Rain (Greek)
- Buddha Lights (Ceylon)
- The Light You Can Hear (Sami)
- Dancing Goats (French)
- The Light of the Northern Dancers, Sacred Cloud, The White Man's Fire, and The Mysterious Fire of the North (Plains tribes)

The Aurora as an Omen

Throughout history, auroras have been associated with major events. The northern lights were seen over London when Germany attacked in 1939 and as far south as Cleveland, Ohio, on December 7, 1941—the date Japan dropped bombs on Pearl Harbor.

In 1583, thousands of French pilgrims prayed for safety after mistaking an aurora for fire in the sky. Throughout the Middle Ages—from 500 to about 1500 AD—people thought auroras were a warning of war or famine. In old Scotland, the aurora meant unpredictable weather or even the birth of a baby. In 1715, James Radcliffe, Earl of Derwentwater, led a rebellion to restore King James to England's throne. The rebellion failed and the Earl was beheaded in the Tower of London. On the night he died, the northern lights glowed in tones of red. This led people in his home region to refer to auroras as Lord Derwentwater's Lights.

Ancient Chinese also thought auroras predicted special events. A woman named Fu Pao watched an aurora take the form of a gigantic dragon one night in 2600 BC. The next day she learned she was pregnant and people predicted her child would become an important ruler. The dragon became a royal symbol and her

Credit: Kevin Thompson

Superstitions

- When auroras are low in the sky, do not whistle. You will not live long if you breathe in the lights. (Sahtu, Northwest Territories)

- Always wear your hat outside, or the lights might burn your hair. (Sami, northern Scandinavia)

- Come home before it gets dark. The lights steal young people away, and the colored lights come from missing children's parkas. (Yupik, Alaska)

son grew up to become the Yellow Emperor, Shuan-Yuan. Some people think the idea of fire-breathing dragons may have come from early aurora watchers.

In Wisconsin, members of the Meskwaki tribes saw auroras as signs of war and disease. They thought the lights in the sky were the ghosts of enemies they had killed, and that their spirits were coming back for revenge. The Meskwaki also believed auroras meant their next battle would be difficult.

The Dene Tha' in northern Alberta considered auroras to be a living force, with unusual colors and patterns suggesting good or bad omens. They believed they could encourage the lights to dance, move more quickly, or disappear by rubbing their fingernails, clapping, or whistling. When cold weather occurred, they said it was caused by the northern lights eating the clouds.

In winter, the Blackfoot in North America predicted violent winds would come after seeing an aurora, which they called "fires of the Northmen."

The Aurora as Fire

The Algonquin people originally lived in the area formed by present-day Ontario and Quebec. One Algonquin legend tells of a demigod called Nanabozho, who created the world and its people. The god decided to make his own home in the Far North, but promised to look after his people, even though he would be so far away. Whenever Nanabozho wanted to show he had not forgotten his pledge, he lit great fires in the sky. The people saw the fires' reflection and knew they could trust the creator to look after them.

In North Dakota, the Mandan tribe described auroras as fires tended by great medicine men and warriors, who used the flames to cook their dead enemies in giant pots. The Menominee in Wisconsin, on the other hand, enjoyed a friendlier outlook. They saw auroras as torches held by kindly giants called manabai'wok—the spirits of great hunters and fishers in the northern regions, who traveled the heavens and speared fish at night. In Washington, members of the Makah tribes thought the lights were fires in the distant north that a tribe of dwarfs used to boil blubber. The dwarfs were supposed to be half the length of a canoe paddle but strong enough to catch whales with only their hands. Aboriginal people on Canada's Vancouver Island had a similar story. They described auroras as the fires of a tribe who boiled blubber on the ice near the North Pole.

The Chippewa explained auroras as glowing fires lit by the ghosts of heroic fighters, while Aboriginal people in maritime Canada supposed they were the glowing embers from a celestial campfire, fed by a giant. The giant was also believed to be responsible for making fog, wind, and meteors.

Inuit from Labrador thought the sky was a large dome that curved around the Earth. Spirits from Earth were said to travel along a narrow path over a deep hole at the end of the world, to reach the heavens through a small opening in the sky. Only the Raven and people who had died a voluntary or violent death could go to this wonderful place where food was plentiful and disease and pain did not exist. Spirits that were already in the sky

Credit: Jimmy Westlake

lit torches to help the new souls find their way, and these lights were seen on Earth as the aurora. Labrador Inuit in Canada thought the spirits whispered with soft crackling and hissing voices that encouraged souls to follow the torchbearers into the heavens. They said whispering back could make the lights come closer and cause you to be captured. For this reason, many feared auroras and hid when its colors decorated the sky.

In the Southern Hemisphere, New Zealand's Maoris also saw auroras. They thought the lights were the reflection of flames from massive fires built by their ancestors in Antarctica.

The emperor Tiberius, who ruled Rome from 14 to 37 AD, saw a red glow in the sky and thought a seaport was on fire. When he sent his army to fight the flames, they arrived to find the port safe but the sky filled with a colorful glimmering aurora.

Auroral Height and Color

The atmosphere becomes very thin 52 miles (85 kilometers) above the Earth's surface. Auroras usually occur from 60 to 620 miles (97 to 1,000 kilometers) up—an area considered outer space.

Auroras can stretch thousands of miles across the sky. They change color as charged particles from the Sun strike different types of gas in Earth's upper atmosphere. Their color also depends on how quickly the Sun's particles travel and the height at which particles and gas collide.

An aurora will appear white if its light is not intense enough for the human eyes to detect its color. Digital cameras are more sensitive to red light than the human eye and photographs have shown red auroras that the eye did not detect, at the top and bottom of green auroras.

Auroras form a variety of shapes including the most commonly seen—bands, arcs, curtains, and spikes. A band of light may divide into multiple strips that ripple, fold, and swirl in changing colors and patterns. Arcs of light can extend across the sky or form curtains that wave and dance, sometimes slowly, other times with increasing speed. Occasionally, multicolored rays will stream outward from a circle of light.

ELEMENT IN EARTH'S ATMOSPHERE	APPROXIMATE ALTITUDES	LIGHT COLOR
Oxygen	60–95 miles (100–150 kilometers)	Green (most common)
Oxygen	95 miles (150 kilometers) and up	Red fringe at the top of a green aurora
Nitrogen	45–60 miles (70–100 kilometers)	Red fringe at the bottom of a green aurora

Aurora Dancers

n the lower Yukon River, Inuit viewed the northern lights as dancing animal spirits such as beluga whales, deer, seal, and salmon. The Inuit of Alaska and Canada thought the lights were caused by the happy dancing of dead souls in the highest level of the afterlife. In Eastern Canada, the Salteaus tribes and Kwakiutl and Tlingit peoples of southeast Alaska also described auroras as the dancing spirits of people who had died. North American Cree tribes saw the lights as the dancing spirits of their ancestors, and claimed that the bright-colored lights meant that the spirits were especially cheerful.

Credit: Sebastian Saarloos

The early Scots gave auroras the charming name "nimble men" as well as na fir-chlis, which means "merry dancers." An old Gaelic proverb warned, "When the mirrie dancers play, they are like to slay." According to legend, the playful dancers sometimes fought over a beautiful maiden. The Scots said you could tell when a fight had occurred because a red-tinted cloud would appear, colored by the aurora. The cloud was considered a pool of fairy blood, and red lichens growing on stones were said to be the blood of the merry dancers.

Auroral Movement

- Auroras appear to rise, dip, and dance in the sky as magnetic and electrical forces react together in lively, constantly shifting combinations.

- Auroral bands of light may have rays that stretch upward. These rays show us where magnetic field lines extend into the atmosphere.

- The calm period before auroras begin to move is called the growth phase. The period when they change from a single slow moving arc to many moving forms is referred to as the substorm onset. When auroras move very quickly it is called the breakup phase, and patchy auroras that pulsate are described as being in the recovery phase.

Credit: Sebastian Saarloos

Sky Spirits

(INUIT)

The early Inuit people living in different parts of the Arctic had a variety of beliefs about the aurora. They often linked it to death and the afterlife. Many watched the auroras' changing colors and dipping lights and believed they were seeing the souls of people who had died, or the dancing souls of animal spirits. In some areas, young people danced to the northern lights. They called the sky spirits selamiut (sky-dwellers).

Inuit who lived along Point Barrow were afraid of the unpredictable lights. They waved sharp knives at the sky and hid their children when auroras lit up the night. Some said throwing dog-doo at an aurora would provide protection. Inuit in other areas thought the mysterious glow should be treated with great respect, believing the lights controlled the weather and their game supply.

Some Inuit used the northern lights to encourage children to go home before the Sun set. They believed an aurora would come closer if you whistled at it. Parents told their children that if the lights heard someone whistling, they would come down and burn them up or cut off their heads.

Inuit along the Bering Sea, as well as in Greenland and northern Canada, had a playful explanation for auroras. They saw the lights as a great game in heaven played by the spirits of children and adults, who used a walrus head or skull for a ball to kick back and forth, like a great soccer game in the sky. The shifting lights showed the movement of the spirits as they struggled to get the ball. The Inuit of Nunivak Island claimed the lights were walrus spirits playing with a human skull!

In Greenland, Inuit said that children who died at birth or were murdered became spirits seen as the northern lights. These unfortunate children were said to be playing with balls made of their own afterbirth (the matter released by a mother's body after a baby is

Auroral Sound

- Some people have heard faint crackling, swishing, and hissing sounds when watching a very bright aurora. That sound cannot have been generated where the light originates because sound travels much slower than light. While light reaches an observer almost instantly, sound takes several minutes to travel the same distance. Noises generated where auroras form could only be heard after seeing the lights.

- In 2012, scientists recorded auroral sounds for the first time. An explanation is not yet known, but it has been suggested that an electromagnetic particle traveling at the speed of light may somehow generate sound near an observer on the ground.

born). The lights moved and changed shape as the children played, skipped, and danced across the night sky.

Some people believe they can hear whistling sounds from auroras. The Inuit explained such sounds by claiming the spirits were trying to communicate with people on Earth. They also believed they could call an aurora when they wanted to send a message to a dead soul, but they only spoke to the aurora with whispering voices.

According to Inuit beliefs, a person's soul would go to different levels of the next world depending on two things: how the person behaved during life, and the cause of their death. Some Inuit believed the highest level of heaven was where auroras were seen. It was a bright, pleasant place without snow or storms, and the animals that lived there were easy to catch.

To achieve this level of heaven, a person had to always help anyone who was poor or starving. A woman who died during childbirth was also expected to reach the top part of heaven, as were individuals who died hunting, were murdered, or had taken their own lives. In Inuit tradition, suicide was seen as a noble act when committed by older people who could no longer contribute to their family's survival. It freed others from the need to care for them.

Some Inuit believed the underworld was actually a better place than the world above,

Credit: Heidi Ferguson, Simply Captured Photography.

where the auroras shone. They felt the underworld was a warm place with plenty of food, while the upper world was cold and miserable, with little to eat. People in the upper world were called the arssartut, meaning ball-players.

The upper world was said to extend up from the Earth's mountains, but the souls who left Earth had to pass through the air to reach it. A man in his kayak was once believed to have reached the upper world by paddling to the ocean's edge, where the water meets the sky.

Skirnir's Journey

(NORSE)

Odin, the highest and wisest of the Norse gods, was the god of war, death, poetry, and wisdom. He was married to Freya, the goddess of love. One day, Odin rode off on his winged, eight-legged horse, Sleipnir, but did not return home. After many days of waiting and watching for her husband, Freya began to cry. Tears of gold fell from her eyes. Frustrated with worry, she felt unable to sit still for another moment. The goddess transformed herself into a falcon by putting on her cloak of feathers and flew off to search for Odin.

Freya was a kind goddess and her brother, Frey, missed her terribly. Frey was a god of peace, as well as a courageous warrior and chief of the group of gods and goddesses of ancient Norway, called the Vanir. These masters of magic were believed to give health, youth, fertility, luck, and riches. They lived in Vanaheim—one of the nine worlds at the top of the universe.

The god of the Sun and the rain, Frey was the most handsome of the Vanir and ruler of the elves. He wanted to be sure his sister was safe and wondered if he should risk climbing Odin's watchtower and sitting in his throne. From there he would be able to see the entire world and everyone in it. As no other god had ever dared to climb the tower, he was sure something horrible and frightening would happen if he took this chance. Still, Frey needed to see his sister and know for himself she was well.

He began to climb the winding steps. Higher and higher he rose, over the stone wall that protected the realm of Asgard and above the clouds toward the sky. At last he reached the tower door, guarded by two grey and hulking wolves—Geri and Freki. The wolves growled at Frey and began to inch toward the god, one on his right and one on his left, as if to edge him backwards down the stone steps.

"Step aside!" Frey commanded, pointing toward the wall. When the wolves heard Frey's voice, they recognized him as a god. Growling more softly, Geri and Freki backed away, forced to let him pass.

Frey opened the watchtower door and stood before Odin's glittering throne. He wondered what fate might befall him if he actually sat upon the sacred chair.

"Odin is the highest god with the greatest magic. He will know his throne has been touched and will punish me." Frey's shoulders sagged.

Had he come this far to change his mind? He so badly wanted to see his sister. Frey stared at the sparkling jewels imbedded in gold on the chair's arms. "A throne is only a chair. Why should I think I will suffer just from sitting in a chair? Should Odin be the only one to view the world from here? Why should I not be allowed to see my sister?"

Before he could talk himself out of it, Frey turned about and sat down in the chair. Immediately the entire world appeared before him. In the upper world, he saw all of Asgard, Vanaheim, and the part he ruled—Alfheim, land of the light elves. He saw Midgard, the middle world where the humans lived, and Nidavellir—land of the dwarfs. Frey looked down into Jotunheim, the snowy mountains where the frost giants lived. He searched Svartalfheim, domain of the dark elves. His eyes swept across the many lands until he finally spotted Freya, looking well and walking in the direction of home.

Now content, Frey was about to rise from the chair when a movement in the land of the giants made him look downward once more. He stared down in the snowy expanse, wondering what had caught his eye, when he saw the door of a house open. A frost giant stepped into the doorway. She was startlingly beautiful, with fair skin that radiated a light so powerful, it rose and danced in the sky before fading away. Frey gazed at the maiden in awe, but not for long. The giant looked out the door for only a moment before turning back inside and shutting the door behind her.

At first Frey had wanted only to see his sister. Now he longed for the frost maiden with a need one hundred times as strong. The god leapt from the chair, raced past the wolves, down the steps, and back into Asgard. He tried to push the image of the frost maiden from his mind by dining with the other gods and goddesses, but found no one whose company could make him forget the site of the beautiful frost giant. Frey left his companions early that evening and tried to sleep but rest would not come. When his eyes finally stayed closed, Frey dreamt he was dancing through the sky with the maiden as her light streamed around them.

By morning, Frey was more tired than if he had not slept at all. He decided to return to the chair and see if he might spot the maiden

Credit: ESA/IPEV/PNRA–B. Healey

again. Perhaps he could find out her name. Frey climbed the stairway, which seemed even more endless than it had the day before. Finally he reached the door to the watchtower, where Geri and Freki growled and snapped. Once again, Frey ordered the beasts to step aside but this time they only stepped closer, nipping at his cloak. Frey realized Odin's chair had worked some magic. He would not be allowed to sit on the throne again, and his fate must be to forever long for the beautiful snow giant.

Poor Frey would not give up. He descended the stairs and sought out his father, Njord, god of wind, sea, and fire. Frey explained how he had come to spot the beautiful frost giant from the watchtower.

"How can I find out the maiden's name?" asked Frey.

"She is Gerda, the daughter of the giant Gymer," said Njord. "You must forget about her. The lord of the elves cannot marry the daughter of a frost giant. Her heart is surely cold and hard. No good will come of it."

"But why?" Frey persisted, overjoyed just to know her name. "Why should love not be a good thing?"

"Odin's punishment will not end with love," said Njord. "The only way you could make Odin's magic work in your favor would be to give up your dearest possession."

"I would give up my magic sword to have Gerda for my wife," insisted Frey.

Njord paled. "You cannot give up your magic sword," he spoke sternly. "Have you forgotten Ragnarok—the final battle that will end our worlds? You may be a god of peace, as well as a brave warrior, but you will still need your sword's protection when war comes."

"Ragnarok will not happen for a very long time," Frey answered. "I would give up my sword if it meant I could be with Gerda." He turned from his father and returned to Alfheim.

Frey was unable to think of anything but winning Gerda. His distraction was so great that he often forgot what he was doing or saying. The other gods and goddesses worried he would not overcome his misfortune. Even nature felt badly for Frey. Birds no longer sang, leaves turned yellow and fell to the ground, and insects stopped humming.

Finally Njord could stand the moping no more. He searched for Frey's shield bearer, Skirnir, and found him polishing his son's shield. Njord asked him to find some way to help Frey. Skirnir was a faithful servant, as well as Frey's friend. Agreeing to try, he set down the shield, and went off to seek him out. Skirnir found his master leaning against a tree, gazing into the swirling waters of a stream.

"You have been very sad, this past while," said Skirnir, sitting down beside his friend. "Is there something I can do to help you?"

Frey told him about sitting in Odin's chair and how he had fallen in love with a frost giant. "I cannot leave the elves to woo my love," said Frey. "If only there was a way for me to tell her how I feel."

"I will go for you," said Skirnir, "but you must lend me your horse and promise me a reward if I am successful."

"I will give you my boat Skidbladnir or my boar Golden Bristle," said Frey.

But Skirnir refused. "I need a weapon," he insisted. "Something that will protect me from the frost giants and trolls. Give me your sword and I will go."

Frey remembered his father's words. Again he told himself that Ragnarok was far in the future. "Take my sword and win Gerda's love for me," said Frey, unbuckling the sword from his side. "Go at once!"

Skirnir ran to get Frey's horse. Bloodyhoof was a powerful animal who could make the ground tremble with his hoof beats and spring unharmed through fire. Skinir leaped onto the horse's back, holding the reins in one hand and Frey's sword in the other. As he galloped forth, wolves and trolls tried to tear him from Bloodyhoof's back, but he plunged the sword toward their snarling faces and they backed away in fear. Approaching the snowy mountains, Skinir could feel the heat from the great wall of flames that stopped most from entering Jotunheim, but Bloodyhoof did not falter. Skirnir raced onward through the flames until finally he saw Gerda's home. Barking dogs announced his arrival as he entered the courtyard. A servant stepped out and asked him his business.

"I must speak to Gerda and no other," said Skirnir, and the maiden led him to a great hall, where Gerda received him.

"I am here to deliver a message to you from my master, Frey, chief of the Vanir. He sends his love and wishes to marry you." Skirnir held out the gifts Frey had sent with him. "Agree to be his bride and you shall have these eleven golden apples and this ring."

Gerda looked at Skirnir with scorn. "I have no need of gold for I have plenty, and I have no need of Frey's love either. Go and do not return. I do not wish to wed."

"Agree to marry Frey or I shall cut off your head with this sword!" Frey stepped closer and raised the sword high. Gerda did not flinch. "I will not marry for gold and I will not marry to save my life."

The frost maiden glared at Skirnir until he began to draw a pattern in the air with the sword. "If you won't marry Frey, I shall cast a spell that will turn you into a revolting witch. Your hair will become gray, your smooth skin wrinkled, your bones bent and crooked. Not even a troll will want your hand in marriage." The magic sword glittered, sparked, and crackled as Skirnir began to cast his spell.

Seeing the sword spark and hearing it sputter frightened Gerda as much as Skirnir's words. "Take away your spell! I shall marry Frey."

Skirnir paused, holding the sword in midair. "When shall you meet and marry him? I must hear you promise. Give me your word!"

"I will marry him nine days hence. Tell him to meet me at Barre, the sacred barley patch. I give me your word. Now go!"

Skirnir turned Bloodyhoof and thundered back to Alfheim. He was happy for Frey and pleased for himself. He could keep the magic sword!

Frey paced his hall until he felt the ground tremble and saw Bloodyhoof come into sight. He ran toward Skirnir, who halted in front of him and prepared to dismount. But Frey could not wait. "Tell me what happened!" he shouted, "What did she say?"

"She will marry you in nine days at Barre," answered Skirnir.

"Nine days!" cried Frey, "How will I ever wait so long?"

Though it felt like nine months of endless winter to Frey, the time did pass. Gerda kept her promise and married Frey in the sacred barley patch. At last content, the god wrapped his arms around Gerda and his love melted away the cold of the frost maiden. She found herself loving him in return. Frey celebrated by giving the Earth sunshine and rain until it shone with splendid colors and a bountiful harvest. The birds sang, insects hummed, and flowers blossomed. And when beautiful Gerda raised her naked arms to the sky, lights rose, danced, and played high above the Earth—forming the remarkable auroras that still awe people today.

Views from Outer Space

- Auroras are seen in ring-shaped areas of the sky called auroral ovals. They are located around Earth's north and south magnetic poles, near the Arctic and Antarctic circles.

- Each of the ovals is about 2,500 miles (4,000 kilometers) in diameter. Their sizes will change from hour to hour and night to night, depending on solar activity.

- An entire auroral oval can only be seen from outer space. Astronauts in the International Space Station (ISS) study auroras—from 250 miles (400 kilometers) above Earth's surface. Satellites with sensitive cameras are also used to observe auroras from space, while space probes allow scientists to detect solar wind and measure the energy and speed of its particles.

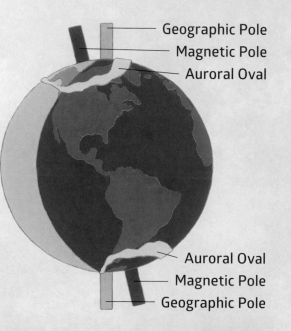

Geographic Pole
Magnetic Pole
Auroral Oval

Auroral Oval
Magnetic Pole
Geographic Pole

Credit: NASA/UC Berkeley

The Valkyries

(NORSE)

n Norse mythology, the world is predicted to end in a battle against the frost giants. The time of this final encounter is called Ragnarok. The gods and goddesses will know Ragnarok is coming because it will follow Fimbulvetr—a severe freezing and stormy winter, more intense than any bleak, bitter, wintry weather ever felt. Snow will fall and wind will bluster for three winters in a row, with no other seasons between. Everyone will begin to argue and hold grudges against one another. It is the sign the end is upon them.

Ragnarok will arrive in full force when the wolf called Skoll eats the Sun and his brother, Hati, swallows the Moon. The stars will disappear from the sky and the world will be black.

The final battle will be fought on the giant plain of Vigrid, which means "battle shaker." All the gods, giants, dwarves, demons, and elves are destined to take part. The great battle will destroy the Earth and finally end when the Earth sinks into the sea. Although it will be the end of the fighting, it will not be the end of all life. Eventually the Earth shall rise out of the ocean—a clean, fresh, new world, and the gods and mortals who survive will live together in peace.

Father of all the gods, Odin, wanted to be ready for the coming of Ragnarok. He knew he would need many soldiers to help him fight this great battle against the frost giants and called upon the Valkyries to help him build his forces. The Valkyries were wildly beautiful female warriors who served Odin as messengers. Carrying spears, they sailed across the sky on winged horses, dressed in shining helmets and sparkling armor.

Odin told the Valkyries to watch the battlefields on Earth for the bravest heroes who had been slain. The Valkyries chose the most courageous soldiers and carried them through the air to Asgard, home of the warrior gods known as the Aesir.

Surrounded by a great stone wall, Asgard

was the highest of the nine Norse worlds. The Valkyries led the warriors to Odin's great hall, called Valhalla, and here they waited for the coming of Ragnarok. Throughout the days, the soldiers from Earth, called the Einherjar, trained in mock battles where they scratched and slashed at each other as if truly facing the enemy. Fortunately, the food and drink they shared at Odin's table healed their wounds completely. All scars, bruises, and other signs they had been hurt were always gone the very next day.

Soldiers from Earth felt honored to be chosen by the Valkyries. Only those about to die in battle could see the maiden warriors and it was said a soldier who dreamt of the Valkyries the night before a skirmish would be chosen the following day. When not dressed in armor, the Valkyries wore cloaks made of swan feathers.

In the Middle Ages, when the Norwegian pirates, called vikings, looked up to see the northern lights dancing in the sky, they claimed the Valkyries were out. They said the auroras were caused by the glistening of Valkyries' armor and the reflections from their shields as they rode at night, running

- Valkyrie means "chooser of the slain."

- Ragnarok, which means "doom of the powers," is also called Gotterdammerung.

- Wednesday is named after Odin, who is also referred to as "Wodan," while Thursday is named after Thor, and Friday takes its name from Odin's wife, Frigg, also known as Freya.

errands for Odin and carrying slain warriors to Valhalla.

The vikings also claimed the lights were the reflection of the ceiling in Valhalla, which was built out of the Valkyries' battle shields. When the vikings saw a red-tinted aurora, they claimed it came from blood that dripped off the sword belonging to Odin's son, the red-bearded Thor—god of thunder.

Eos' Wish

(GREEK)

Eos, the Greek goddess of the dawn, helped bring light to the world each day. Her job was to open the gates of the East for her brother, Helios, the Sun god. Every day, Helios journeyed across the sky, steering the four wild and winged horses that pulled the fiery chariot of the Sun.

One morning, Eos pushed the heavy Gates of the East outward and watched as light filtered through the doorway in a striking blend of colors.

"'Tis nearly morning," she called into Helios's chamber. "Arise and prepare for your journey. Pyrois, Aeos, Aethon and Phlegon prance before your chariot. They are anxious for you to guide them across the sky. Awaken, dear brother."

Handsome Helios stepped out of his room in a billowing robe that shimmered with all the colors of the rainbow. He took the reins from a servant and stepped into the brilliant, gleaming chariot. With a fond wave to Eos, Helios guided the horses upward and the stars that had glittered in the black night began to fade. The heavens turned a pale blue-gray until a pastel yellow glow overtook the sky, finally turning to a deep gold that became orange, then red, edged with rays of purple light.

The birds on Earth began to sing their morning songs. Roosters crowed, animals stretched in patches of sunshine, and light-loving insects crawled from nighttime hiding places. Finally the sky became a dazzling robin-egg blue tinted with gold as Helios's chariot passed through the gate on his path towards the western ocean.

On Earth, Tithonus rose before sunrise each day so that he could catch a glimpse of the goddess of the dawn. A mortal, Tithonus was the son of Laomedon, the king of Troy. Tithonus felt especially cheerful on the days he was able to spot the beautiful and young Eos as she swung open the eastern palace

Forecasting Auroras

· Astronomers try to forecast when auroras might develop by observing the Sun's activity, but so far auroral forecasts are less reliable than weather predictions.

· Scientists observing flares and coronal mass ejections can predict auroras two to three days before they occur because solar wind takes that long to reach Earth.

· The brightness of auroras can be predicted one to two hours ahead of time using solar wind information collected by satellites.

· Scientists estimate the size of the auroral oval to determine what latitude an aurora is likely to reach, as well as the time—within a few hours—when it may be seen.

Credit: Jimmy Westlake

· If you see a dim, spread-out aurora slowly moving south, you can predict the auroral breakup will occur in a few minutes.

gates. Eos welcomed each day with gladness but always disappeared inside very quickly. Tithonus wished he could see the goddess for longer. He did not know that Eos chose to slumber through the day to avoid seeing the troubles in the world.

One day Eos opened the gates for Helios but did not rush off to sleep. The open entryway created a glorious sunrise that lasted on and on. She glanced down at the Earth and wondered if she might be missing anything pleasant by sleeping every day. Just as this thought occurred to her, Eos spotted Tithonus gazing upwards in adoration and had her answer.

The lovestruck Eos took Tithonus to Ethiopia, where they enjoyed great happiness in each other's company and had two children—Memnon and Emathion.

Despite her happiness, Eos feared the future. She knew that as a goddess she would live forever but Tithonus could only live a human lifetime. Unable to imagine life without the man she loved, she decided to ask Zeus, king of the gods, to grant Tithonus the gift of immortality. If he agreed, Tithonus would live forever and they could always be together.

The next day, Eos woke Helios and rushed him out the door, causing a rather windy morning. She made her way to Mount Olympus where the great gods lived and searched for Zeus. She spotted the regal god grasping a thunderbolt on the side of the mountain and ran up to him so fast that her breath was reduced to shorts gasps. Despite Zeus's imposing figure, Eos did not hesitate to make her request.

"Oh, grand king of all the gods," Eos implored. "I have come to ask a special favor, for I love the mortal Tithonus and wish to be with him for all time. Please honor me by granting him immortality so that we may be together forevermore."

Zeus looked at Eos. "Are you sure happiness will be yours if I agree to this wish?" asked Zeus. "You must think carefully before asking for such a longing to be made real."

"I am sure," insisted Eos, though she had considered the idea for fewer hours than there are in a day. After all, what could go wrong spending eternity with the object of her desire?

"Be certain," commanded Zeus, watching Eos carefully. "For once a man is made immortal, he cannot die. The wish cannot be undone."

"I am certain," said Eos, her heart thudding faster as she imagined Zeus might really give Tithonus the gift of living forever.

"It is done," said Zeus. "But do not complain to me if you tire of him."

"I promise and I thank you!" Eos exclaimed, her smile brilliant and eyes glittering with excitement. How easy it had been to ensure her love would be with her always! Eos did not spare a moment to wonder why Zeus might have cautioned her to wish carefully. She rushed home to tell Tithonus the good news.

The years passed, happy days filled with joy, laughter, and love. But as more and more time went by, Eos was forced to watch helplessly as Tithonus turned from the handsome and spirited young man she had fallen in love with to a very old, wrinkled, and slow-moving man. His hair grew grey, his bones became stiff, and his speech turned gruff and slow. Tithonus became too stooped over to dance, too impatient for parties, and too irritable for laughter.

Finally a day came when he could not even rise from his bed to admire the beautiful sunrise Eos had created. More than anything he had endured, this made Tithonus long for some relief from the daily suffering of old age. The goddess also yearned for some solution, but neither could think what to do.

Eos felt foolish for not paying attention when Zeus warned her to take care before asking him to grant such a wish. An immortal being, Eos would always remain in the same young body and keep her light-hearted spirit. But as a mortal, Tithonus would age with each passing moment, though as Zeus promised, he would never die.

Eons passed and Tithonus's body continued to show the passage of time. His stooped back lurched further downward and he could no longer straighten his spindly legs. The skin on his face and arms turned brown from the Sun for sometimes he did not even have the strength to seek cool shade. His once deep voice lost its luster and his mind became befuddled from too many years of thinking. Tithonus began to repeat himself, constantly uttering a chirping sound. The poor, old man had shrunk into a grasshopper—a grasshopper that would live forever.

Eos watched as the one she had once adored hopped away. She did not try to stop him, for a goddess cannot be married to an insect. Over time, the goddess of the dawn had other husbands, as well as children. Four of her sons were the north, south, east, and west winds. One son was killed and when she thinks of him, her tears form the morning dew.

More than 2000 years ago, the ancient Romans conquered the Greeks. They accepted the Greek myths as their own but changed the names of the gods and goddesses. Eos became known as Aurora—the name now used to describe the glowing lights that dip, dart, and dance like an elegant ballet in the black sky.

The Rainbow Belt

(WABANAKI/ALGONQUIN)

Chief Morning Star and his wife worried about their only son, for he did not like to spend time with children his own age. In fact, he behaved very differently from the other boys in their tribe. Sometimes the boy took his bow and arrow and left the safety of the camp for days at a time. He never said where he was going or when he might return. He never talked about where he had been, even when they asked him, "Where did you go? What did you see when you were away?"

The chief did not like being ignored when he asked his son a question and decided to watch the boy more carefully. Like a warrior on the hunt, the chief blended into the landscape, his eyes following every movement and detail of his son's actions. He noticed the boy always carried his bow and arrows and walked north when he disappeared on one of his mysterious trips.

One day, when the boy took his bow and arrow up the trail northward, the chief told his wife, "I am going to find out what our son is up to."

She was afraid some harm would come to him but knew he must go.

"Return to me safely," she said softly and watched as he followed the boy's path.

The chief tracked the boy through the woods, then up and up the gently sloping land. He stayed far enough back to avoid being seen, but close enough to never lose sight. They walked for such a long time that the land began to change. The trees became stunted and twisted. Soil gave way to rock, eventually changing from dark to lighter shades until the trail they followed was completely white.

The chief had never been this way before. He began to feel odd, almost light-headed with each passing step. The feeling became stronger until he felt himself rising into the air. At the same time, his memory slipped away. Helpless to what was happening, the chief's eyes closed and he remembered no more.

Morning Star did not know how much time had passed when the odd feeling began to finally disappear. He opened his eyes and saw that he stood in a strange land bathed in a radiant glow. It was different from daylight, moonlight, starlight, firelight, or any light he had ever seen. The chief looked up into the sky but saw no Sun, no Moon, no stars. He looked around for his son and was startled to see a group of people nearby. They looked somehow different from the people in his own tribe, but he could not say how. He searched their faces for his son, but could not find the boy. The chief saw the people looking at him with friendly faces and felt relieved they did not want to harm him. He walked toward the group.

"I am here to find my son," said the chief. "Have you seen a boy that does not belong to your tribe?"

A man stepped forward and answered Morning Star, but he spoke using words the chief did not understand. Morning Star walked up to another group of people. "I am here to find my son," said the chief. "Have you seen a boy that does not belong to your tribe?"

Again a man stepped forward, but this time he spoke in Morning Star's language.

"Are you lost?" he asked. "Do you know where you are?"

"I do not know where I am," said the chief. "But it is not a mistake that I am here. I was following my son but now I cannot see him."

"I know who your son must be," said the man. "Every now and then a visitor comes from the lower land to play ball with our people. You will see him soon."

"But where am I?" asked Morning Star.

"This is the land of the Wa-ba-ban—the northern lights."

Now the chief knew what caused the strange light. He looked around in wonder. The man watched him curiously.

"Did you have a strange feeling as you traveled here? Did you begin to forget what you were doing and why you had come?" asked the man. "That is how it was for me when I first came here from the lower country."

"Yes," answered the chief. "That is how it was for me too. I felt my spirit rising and my memory slipping away. Yet now I remember."

"You must have followed your son along the trail of the Milky Way. That is the only way here," said the man. "It is called Ket-á-gus-wowt—the Spirits' Path."

"How do I get home again?" asked Morning Star. "I must take my son back with me."

"The chief of the northern lights can help you return to your homeland," said the man. "I will talk to him after you see your son play ball."

As he spoke, the players began to gather for the game. Morning Star stared in

Environmental Effects

- Seen as auroras, geomagnetic substorms send great amounts of energetic electrons toward the Earth. This surge of magnetic energy in our atmosphere can cause problems such as power blackouts, satellite and spacecraft damage, radio interference, and navigation system problems. Magnetic disruptions can also expose astronauts in space to radiation. Ham radio operators may have problems sending radio signals during an aurora.

- At heights of 60 to 125 miles (100 to 200 kilometers) above the Earth, temperatures near auroras may multiply tenfold and winds can blow at more than 1000 miles (1,600 kilometers per hour).

Credit: Sebastian Saarloos

astonishment as the players placed shining bands around their heads and glowing belts around their waists.

"Those are called Menquan," said the man. "They are rainbow belts."

The players began to toss a ball back and forth. Every time someone touched the ball, tinted streams of light burst forth from the players' heads and waists in outpourings of color that danced and twirled and hung in shimmering sheets against the sky. As soon as the first streak of light crossed overhead, more braves stepped out of white wigwams to join the fun.

The chief watched in wonder and noticed the rainbow lights that streamed from one young player were more brilliant than anyone else's. With a start, he realized he was admiring his own son! White, then green, yellow, purple, and red wisps of light flared from the boy.

As Morning Star watched the game, the man who had spoken to him slipped away to talk to the leader of the people who lived in the Land of the Northern Lights. He walked up to a brilliant white wigwam and called out, "A chief is here from the lower country. His name is Morning Star and he seeks his son—the boy who comes every few days to play ball. The chief wishes to take the boy home with him."

"We will honor Morning Star's wish," answered the chief of the northern lights.

The chief stepped out of the wigwam and walked to the place where the ball players ran back and forth, shining with light. They stopped playing and looked at one another as they waited for the chief to speak.

"Bid the boy farewell," said the great chief. "Our visitor must return with his father to the land below." The ball players embraced the boy whose colors shone the brightest. When they were done, the chief crooked one finger in the air and two gigantic birds flew to his side.

"Take the chief and his son to their home," he ordered.

The enormous birds jumped in the air, wings flapping. One grasped the chief's shoulders, the other clutched the boy. The birds lifted their passengers into the sky and flew southward. Morning Star and his son knew they had reached the path of the Milky Way when their minds started to drift and their eyes began to droop. They remembered nothing else until they landed back on Earth, next to the chief's wigwam.

The chief's wife was very happy to see her son and husband again. She ran from the wigwam and embraced them both. From that time and on, Morning Star's son stayed on Earth. He taught the men of the Wabanaki tribe to play ball and his parents were pleased to have him near.

Land of Eternal Memory

(MI'KMAQ/FRENCH-CANADIAN)

Long ago, a woman traveled along a deer trail through the forest carrying her infant son. She had picked berries all day and was on her way home when she left the path to pick from one last patch. Collecting as much fruit as she could carry, the woman fed her child and looked for the trail but it was not to be seen. They slept beneath a spruce tree that night, and for half a dozen nights more, before finally finding a cave in a pebbly bank. She carried her son inside, settled him in her arms, and leaned back against the cave's rocky wall. The drumming of rain pouring from the sky soothed them both to sleep.

The sky was faintly lit when the woman woke to the sound of breathing just beyond the cave's entrance. An enormous bear lumbered inside, and the woman pressed back against the wall in fright. She could see by his size that this was the chief of all bears. The bear lay down beside her and placed his head upon her lap. His warmth felt comforting, and the woman laid her hand upon the bear's fur and fell asleep. She woke to see her son crawling along his back.

The three spent the winter inside the cave and the bear grew fond of the boy. His magic made the child age with a mysterious and unusual speed, and that winter he grew from a helpless infant, to a brawny boy, to an incredibly strong young man. The bear and the young man liked to wrestle one another, and after a winter of practice the young man became powerful enough to overcome the massive animal. The bear, the boy, and his mother were pleased, but eventually it was time to think of other things. As the snow melted and the summer birds returned, the woman began to miss her people.

"It is springtime and we must go home," she said, and began to prepare for the journey. The bear led them to the path she had been unable to find in the fall and walked with them for five days. When the village was in sight, they said goodbye and the bear loped back into the forest.

The tribe looked at the boy in awe. They had only been gone one winter! How had the child grown so quickly? The woman told them of the bear chief's friendship and they honored the woman and her son with great respect.

The woman settled back into village life but the boy itched for adventure. One day he sought out his mother and said, "I'm easily the strongest in the village. I want to test my strength in the world beyond our home. Send me with your blessing and I'll come back when I'm done."

The mother packed her son a bundle of food and watched him disappear into the forest. He walked for several days before stopping to rest on a riverbank. Leaning against a rock, the young man heard shouting and looked upriver. A canoe full of people was floating downstream. They had no paddles and called for help when they saw him. But before the young man could jump up, another man on the bank picked up a fallen log. He thrust it beneath the canoe and lifted the boat right out of the water and onto the shore. The young man sped to the canoe, lifted it high in the air, and carried it farther up the shore.

"I see you are as strong as I," he said, walking up to the man who had saved the people. "Join me in my search for another who shares our might."

The man who had lifted the canoe nodded and followed the young man up the river. The land rose into hills, the plants gave way to rocks, and the air became cooler as they walked. Several days later, the pair came upon a man rolling a boulder as large as a wigwam up a steep mountain slope. They watched in silence. Then, the young man dashed up the hill, heaved the rock high, and tossed it to the top of the mountain. The man who had been rolling the stone stared at him in shock.

"We are two strong men, looking for a third," the young man placed his hand on the rock-roller's shoulder. "Join us and we will go hunting for moose."

The man agreed and they searched for a good place to set up camp. The threesome chose a clearing in the mountain valley, built a camp next to a fresh spring, and made plans. Each day, two would leave the camp to hunt while the third stayed behind to prepare the evening meal.

The first day, the man from the river stayed back and cooked venison stew for his comrades. Suddenly, a young boy appeared at the campfire.

"May I have something to eat?" he asked.

The man turned around quickly, for he had not heard anyone coming. Noting the boy's tattered clothes and dirty, uncared for appearance, he dished him some stew and watched him eat. When the man turned his back to add a stick to the fire, the boy reached for the

Magnetic Storms

- A solar magnetic storm will often generate an especially strong solar wind, which can disturb the Earth's magnetic field, and overload the magnetosphere with more energy than it can retain. A substorm occurs when that energy is released and flows back toward Earth's upper atmosphere.

- A substorm will produce exceptionally bright, active auroral displays and cause the auroral oval to grow larger than its usual size. It may last up to a few hours and produce auroras much farther from the polar regions than usual. In North America, substorms have caused auroras to be visible from all of Canada and into areas of the United States where they are not typically seen.

- A single auroral storm can release up to a trillion watts of electricity—enough to run 250 million clothes dryers for one hour.

- NASA's Themis mission studies Earth's auroras and examines why auroras change from slow to fast-moving streaks of light. Finding answers will help scientists better understand Earth's magnetosphere and the Sun-Earth connection.

pot of stew and helped himself to the rest of it. Before the man could say a word, the child gobbled it all up, grinned wickedly, and raced towards the mountain. The man shouted after him, but the boy did not even look back. He disappeared into the hills and the man was forced to explain to the others how he had been tricked. They were not pleased but knew nothing could be done.

The next day, the stone-rolling man stayed back and prepared a wonderful smelling soup. It was gently bubbling over the fire when the ragged child walked up. Tears rolled down his face.

"May I please have a bite to eat?" The man looked at the child's sad eyes and found himself handing the boy a dish of the hearty soup. As the child ate, the man tidied the camping area and turned his back to the boy. When he faced him again, the boy was halfway up the mountain and the cooking pot was empty again! His comrades soon returned, anxious to enjoy a good meal. The cook looked at the ground as he mumbled excuses to his friends and they slept with hollow, growling bellies.

The next night, the young man himself stayed back, vowing no visitor would fool him. To prepare their meal, he wrapped strips of meat over a network of branches near the fire, turning the meat again and again to make sure it cooked evenly. He watched the clearing but did not see the child until he heard his voice.

"May I have a bite to eat, please?" The young man looked at the scraggly child and told him to eat until he was full. He did not turn his back on the boy, so when the meat was gone and the boy tried to race for the mountain, the young man grabbed him by the arm and held him tight. The boy tried to wriggle free and nearly escaped once, for he had strong powers, but in the end he could not get away from his captor—the one who had learned to wrestle from a bear.

"Please set me free!" begged the boy, but the young man held him firm. "Please set me free!" he said again. "If you do I will take you to my home. I serve a terrible seven-headed monster. He has never met a man he did not want to fight or a foe he could not defeat but you are so strong, I think that you could beat him."

"This is exactly the kind of challenge I have wished for," said the young man, "but how do I know this is not a trick to see me die?"

"I will prove my honesty," the boy reached behind him. "Take this stick. It is the only object that can make the giant feel pain."

The young man held the polished stick and felt its power. He released the boy and followed him up the mountain to the entrance of a cave. When they stepped inside, a burly seven-headed giant grabbed the young man by the shoulders and tossed him to the ground. The young man pulled the creature down with him and they wrestled on the cave floor, rolling over rocks, then outside into trees and fallen logs. Soon both were covered with wounds, but they ignored their pain and continued to batter one another, even as twilight approached. The Sun was beginning to sink over the mountain when the young man called to the boy, "fetch me the stick!"

Darting forward, the boy tossed the stick toward the man's outstretched palm then backed his way to safety. The young man's fingers curled around the rough wood. Just as the boy had promised, its magic took hold and he felt his strength renewed. The young man raised the cane to strike the grimacing heads, over and over, until at last the giant was still. Fourteen eyes stared blankly from their faces.

"Because you have spared my life," said the

boy, "you must meet my sisters and choose one for a wife." The young man followed the boy over the mountain to the entrance of another cave. Three beautiful fairy maidens sat around a small fire.

The young man chose the maiden closest to his own age to become his wife and invited the other two to return with him to wed his friends. It was a long walk back around the mountain, but only a short way if they climbed the steep slope above them.

Fortunately, the young man's companions had heard the sounds of fighting and were calling out to the young man. He looked up, and saw they stood above him on the mountain.

"Send a rope down for us," called the young man. "We are each to have a beautiful wife." The two strong men looked down in surprise at their companion, standing below them with three beautiful fairy women. They ran to get a rope, tied one end to a sturdy tree near the cliff, then lowered the rope. The young man sent up the oldest sister, then the middle one.

As his companions once again lowered the rope, the young man decided to test their loyalty. He knew they could not come close enough to the cliff's edge to see what they were lifting. He tied a rock to the rope and shouted, "I'm coming next."

The stone rose higher and higher up the mountainside but when nearly at the top, it crashed down, trailed by a slashed rope. The rock shattered into shards of stone and flakes of dust, spraying the air. To escape injury, the young man and his maiden were forced to duck behind a boulder. Shocked at this violent act, the two fairy sisters at the top of the cliff ran away from the men they were to marry, and their brother cursed the men to chase after his sisters forevermore, never to catch up. The young man was saddened by this betrayal, and never saw his companions again.

The strong young man took his fairy wife into the forest and they spent a happy winter getting to know each other. When spring came, the boy decided it was time to keep his promise to his mother.

"Wait here for me and I will be back in a few days," he said.

"Please do not go," insisted the fairy wife. "You are bound to forget me."

"I must keep my promise to my mother," answered the young man, already gathering his belongings.

"If you must go," said his wife, "heed my words. A small black dog will greet you at your home. When he tries to jump up and lick your hand, step back and be sure he does not touch you. The dog is an evil spirit whose touch will make you forget me."

"I will not let the dog near me," agreed the young man, "and I will be back soon."

He walked to his family's village and just as the fairy had warned, a small black dog jumped toward him. He remembered his wife's warning but before he could step back, the dog

Credit: Heidi Ferguson, Simply Captured Photography

licked his hand. From that point on, he had no memory of the fairy maiden and forgot about returning to her in the forest.

The young man's wife waited for him to return. Almost a month passed before she decided to find out if the dog had succeeded. Letting her fire die low, she walked in the direction he had gone and continued until she reached the edge of the forest near the village. As it was daylight, she hid in the woods and tried to spot her husband.

Peering around the tree trunks, the fairy maiden could not see her husband. She tried to get a better view by climbing an old ash tree. Its branches spread over a pool of water next to a stream. As she sat in the tree, a young woman walked by on her way to collect some water and glanced down into the pool. She saw the reflection of the fairy-wife's face and imagined that some sorcery had made her grow incredibly beautiful.

"I needn't do chores," said the girl with a toss of her head. "Surely a chief's son will want to marry this face." She returned to the village to show off her beauty to the men.

When the young woman did not return with the water she had been sent to fetch, her mother came to the stream to get it herself.

She glanced down into the pool and saw the fairy's reflection.

"I am young again! My beauty has returned!" she exclaimed. "I needn't do chores," said the woman with a toss of her head, "Surely a chief will want to marry this face." She returned to the village to show off her beauty to the men.

Finally an old man came to the stream. He dipped down to drink from the pool of water and saw the reflection of the fairy wife's beautiful face. "That cannot be me," said the old man, "for I have never been fair, nor am I a woman. Who is hiding in this tree?" he asked, dropping the water he had collected.

"I am the wife of the strong young man who has returned to the village," answered the fairy. "Do you know where he is?"

"He has gone hunting upriver," answered the old man, "but he will be back tonight."

"I will wait here," answered the fairy. "Please do not mention that you have seen me."

The old man promised to keep the fairy a secret and brought her some food to eat while she waited. When the shadows began to lengthen, she came down from the tree and walked upriver to look for her husband. Finally she saw a man paddling a canoe on the river—it was him. The fairy began to sing a magical song, and as the young man heard her melody, his memory returned. He was sickened to realize he had forgotten his wife, their happy times, and all that had led them to be together. They embraced in the moonlight.

"We must never part again," said the young man, holding her tight to his chest. The fairy shivered, for she knew they were not yet safe from the dog's evil magic.

"The only way to be sure you will not forget me once more," said the fairy, "is to leave this part of the world where memories can be tricked."

"We will do what you think is best," agreed the young man, for everything she had said had come to pass. "Where can we go?"

"To the Land of Eternal Memory," said the fairy. "It's a place where people can never forget the ones they care about. We can be happy there."

Taking her husband's hands, the fairy began to sing a soft and tender song, her voice rising and falling in a gentle pitch, until a gigantic bird appeared overhead with a wingspan as wide as a pond. It was the mighty Culloo, the leader of all great birds. Soaring towards them, Culloo landed on the ground with a booming whoosh. The fairy climbed onto the bird's back and pulled her husband up to sit behind her. With a thunderous flapping of its wings, the bird sprang into the air and flew up, up, up into the sky.

As the great Culloo lifted them into the heavens, the strong man and his fairy wife felt themselves grow light as they transformed into the aurora. You can still see them, along with their children, in the northern sky—the Land of Eternal Memory. They shiver and shake when they look down and remember the Land of Forgetfulness, then dance across the sky in joy, knowing they will be together for all time.

Searching for Auroras

How to Look for Auroras

For the best viewing, visit a dark site far away from city lights. Give your eyes fifteen to twenty minutes to get used to the darkness. This will allow you to make out weak as well as bright auroras. If you need to look toward a lit area, keep one eye closed so that both eyes will not have to readjust.

Choose a night when the sky is dark and clear because auroras occur high above the clouds. Auroras are not visible in the daytime and moonlight makes them difficult to see. If you are in a place dark enough to see the Milky Way galaxy, it is dark enough to see an aurora.

If solar activity is high, you may see an aurora soon after the Sun has set and the sky has become dark. More often, however, auroras do not appear until later in the evening. In the Northern Hemisphere, they usually begin as a glow on the northeastern horizon.

Sometimes it is hard to tell if you are looking at high clouds or a weak aurora. If you see rapid motion and changes of shape, you will know you are watching the lights.

When to Look for Auroras

Auroras are visible to the unaided eye throughout the year, but are more frequently seen in the spring and fall. March and late September–October are especially good times to look for auroras because Earth's orbit passes through the highest zone of solar activity. Since it is not as cold outside, you will also find aurora-watching a more comfortable pastime during these seasons.

Auroral activity varies greatly and is impossible to predict in detail. An aurora might be visible for an entire night, a few hours, or only minutes. There could be strong auroral activity as the Sun sets, or no activity until several hours later. The strongest activity often occurs within a few hours of local midnight, when the Sun is on the opposite side of Earth from you and the magnetotail is on your side of Earth. Not knowing when or where it will appear is part of what makes spotting auroras fun.

If you see an aurora on a particular evening, the following night will also be a good time to search the night sky. The brightest lights are usually seen in the hours around midnight or later.

After you see a major light show, count twenty-seven nights from that date and look up for another good chance to observe auroras. The Sun rotates every twenty-seven days, causing its active solar regions to send strong solar wind toward the Earth about the same time every month.

The number of spots on the Sun varies during a cycle that lasts from eight to thirteen years. Flares, coronal mass ejections, and other forms of solar activity follow the same sunspot cycle, with more auroras occurring at the cycle's peak. During this period, auroras may also occur at latitudes beyond the ranges where they are usually seen.

Where to Look for Auroras

Auroras are most commonly seen from the Earth's far northern and southern regions. In the Northern Hemisphere, auroras are typically seen from central Alaska and northern Canada, Greenland, and northern Scandinavia and Russia. In the Southern Hemisphere, they are visible over the oceans around Antarctica and sometimes from parts of New Zealand, southern Chile, and Tasmania in Australia.

Solar flares can cause extremely bright auroras and magnetic storms. When solar flares increase the number of particles in Earth's atmosphere, auroras may be spotted beyond the polar regions and toward the equator. They are seen within twenty degrees or so of the equator about once or twice per century.

Auroras are more often observed on the Canadian side of the Northern Hemisphere because the north magnetic pole is in the Canadian Arctic.

Magnetic storms can cause auroras to move southward. Although rarely observed from locations as far south as Florida or Texas, auroras have been seen in many parts of the USA.

Auroras are best seen away from cities and without the interference of light pollution created by artificial lights. If possible, search online for aurora predictions in your area and plan to skygaze from a dark rural site later in the evening.

Visit www.joangalat.com to access links to cool astronomy sites.

Enjoying the Aurora Through Facts and Fiction

The most brilliant light shows are the ones created high in the heavens and seen as aurora. It is no wonder these magical wisps of rising and falling colors have inspired legends, folklore, and superstitions. It's impossible to look up at them without marveling—why do they exist?

Both early peoples and modern science have tried to answer this question. Ancient cultures told stories of spirits, gods, people, and creatures seen high overhead as auroras. Their tales showed connections between the Earth and sky, and characters who could be kind, harsh, wise, or foolish, but never boring. Some legends explained the details people noticed, like why the lights changed colors or moved at different speeds. Others noted the appearance of auroras at important times—such as the birth or death of a person. Linking events on Earth with the events they observed in the sky helped early peoples make sense of their world.

Today, scientists make sense of the world through experimentation and research, as well as observation. Just like the ancient tales, the science of auroras is captivating. Thanks to astronomy, we know the Sun ejects plasma, solar wind sails toward the Earth, and magnetic fields collide. Still, there are always more questions to answer. Astronomers are exploring how the Earth's magnetic field impacts space weather and how it protects our planet, and life on Earth, from charged-particle radiation from the Sun and cosmic rays from deep space.

Science helps us understand the physical aspects of what's happening in the sky, but ancient stories still have a place. They give us a glimpse of historical times and remind us that the wonder of the night sky connects us with peoples past, present, and future. As you gaze upwards on clear, dark nights, think about the Sun-Earth connection and imagine those ancient storytellers who looked up and wondered about the enchanting lights we call the aurora.

Glossary

Atom the smallest unit of an element, made of electrons, protons, and neutrons.

Aurora borealis the name for an aurora in the Northern Hemisphere.

Aurora australis the name for an aurora in the Southern Hemisphere.

Charged particle a small amount of matter with a positive or negative electric charge.

Convection the movement of gas or liquid, where warmer parts move upward and colder parts move downward.

Core the inner, central part of a celestial body.

Corona the Sun's outer atmosphere made of plasma and stretching more than 620,000 miles (1 million kilometers) from the Sun's surface.

Coronal mass ejection a great explosion of hot plasma released by the Sun.

Cosmic rays high-energy charged particles that come from outer space.

Crust the Earth's outermost layer.

Electrical current a flow of positively or negatively charged electric particles, such as electrons.

Electricity the presence and flow of charged particles.

Electromagnetic any phenomenon that involves electricity and magnetism.

Electron a basic particle of matter with a negative electrical charge.

Element a substance made of only one type of atom.

Energetic particle matter that is moving very fast.

Equator an imaginary circle around a planet or moon that divides the north and south hemispheres, midway between the north and south geographic poles.

Flare a sudden increase in brightness on a star, especially on the Sun's surface.

Geomagnetic relating to Earth's magnetism.

Geographic poles the two points, one in the north, one in the south, located at the ends of the Earth's axis of rotation.

Ion an atom or molecule that has gained or lost at least one electron, resulting in a positive or negative charge.

Ionosphere upper part of the atmosphere that stretches upward from about 37 to 620 miles (60 to 1,000 kilometers).

Latitude the distance of a location north or south of the Earth's equator, measured in degrees.

Magnetic field the area around a magnetic body or electric current that has a detectable magnetic force. A magnetic field may extend from the interior of a planetary body and out into surrounding space.

Magnetic pole the region where a magnetic field is strongest. Earth's magnetic poles are the areas, near the north and south geographic poles, where a compass needle will point at a ninety degree angle to the Earth's surface.

Magnetic storm strong solar winds that disturb the magnetosphere.

Magnetosphere region where the influence of Earth's magnetic field is felt. It lies within the ionosphere's uppermost region and reaches about 40,000 miles (64,000 kilometers) into outer space.

Magnetotail the part of the magnetic field that stretches outward on the night side of Earth, pointing away from the Sun.

Magnetopause where the Earth and Sun's magnetic fields meet and have the same strength.

Milky Way galaxy the name of the galaxy where the Earth is located, which appears as a band of light seen across the night sky. It is about 100,000 light years across and contains at least 200 billion stars.

Molecule a particle of matter composed of at least two atoms.

Nuclei the object at the center of an atom that contains most of the mass of the atom and has a positive electrical charge. It contains protons and neutrons.

Particle a small amount of matter, such as a subatomic particle, atom, or molecule.

Photosphere the bright surface layer of the Sun from which light is emitted.

Plasma matter in a state similar to a gas except that the particles are electrically charged.

Particle a very small bit of matter.

Prominence flame-like eruption of gas on the Sun's surface.

Proton a positively charged particle that is a component of the nuclei of atoms.

Radiation the flow of energy from a source that is usually hot. Humans detect solar radiation as heat and visible light.

Satellite an object that orbits a planet, Moon, or star. Natural satellites are celestial objects, while artificial satellites are placed into orbit by scientists to collect information or assist communication.

Subatomic particle a part of matter smaller than an atom, including protons, neutrons, and electrons.

Substorm a disturbance in the magnetosphere, caused by an increase of high-energy particles from the Sun, that causes increased auroral activity.

Space weather the processes and phenomena that occur as a result of the interaction of the solar wind with Earth's magnetosphere.

Sunspot a region on the Sun's surface where the magnetic field is very strong.

Watt a unit used to measure power

Index

About the Author

JOAN MARIE GALAT lives in Alberta's countryside, near Edmonton, where she can be found late in the evening, gazing upwards. She shares her love of the night sky in the *Dot to Dot in the Sky* series, which offers both modern-day astronomy and stories from ancient cultures.

Joan's writing career began with a weekly newspaper column when she was 12. Now an award-winning and bestselling author, she has more than a dozen books, for both children and adults. She provides freelance writing and editing through her communications business, MoonDot Media, and is a frequent presenter at schools and libraries.

The long winter nights and big prairie sky are ideal for stargazing but Joan also enjoys other pastimes such as reading, camping, kayaking, and even stiltwalking. She likes spending time outdoors, picnicking, and traveling, which led to her book *Day Trips From Edmonton*. Her website at www.joangalat.com contains additional author information, astronomy links, and details on her presentations and writing workshops.

Credit: Rob Hislop Photography.

About the Illustrator

LORNA BENNETT was born in Edmonton, Alberta, and attended Grant McEwan College and the University of Alberta in the Fine Arts/Arts faculties.

She has illustrated more than a dozen children's picture books, and many greeting cards, animation projects, book covers, etc. She teaches illustration in schools, libraries, and conferences. Lorna has been a staff artist on the wards at the U of A Hospital for many years, bringing art-making to the bedside of adult patients. Lorna lives in Edmonton.